BROWN BEARS

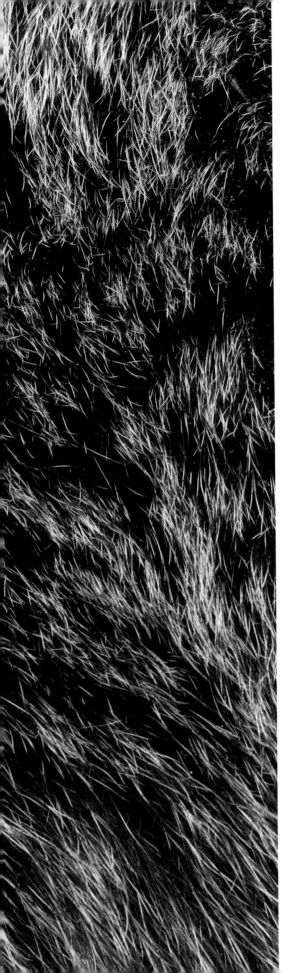

LIVING WILD

Published by Creative Education
P.O. Box 227, Mankato, Minnesota 56002
Creative Education is an imprint of The Creative Company
www.thecreativecompany.us

Design and production by Mary Herrmann
Art direction by Rita Marshall
Printed in the United States of America

Photographs by Alamy (Joe Austin Photography, Moviestore collection Ltd, Radius Images, Richard Sharrocks, Stock Connection Blue), Dreamstime (Lukas Blazek, Mario Bonomi, Jens Klingebiel, Melonstone, David Persson, Branimir Ritonja), Getty Images (Grant Faint, Ngaire Lawson, Paul Souders, David Tipling), iStockphoto (BostjanT, ewanchesser, herreid14), Shutterstock (AMA, Galyna Andrushko, Tatiana Belova, BGSmith, Horia Bogdan, Jim David, Anton Derevschuk, Mat Hayward, Sergey Krasnoshchokov, Eduard Kyslynskyy, a. v. ley, Jim Lopes, Manamana, Erik Mandre, Mighty Sequoia Studio, Nagel Photography, Peterson-Media, PhotoBarmaley, Igor Shootov, spirit of america, Miki Verebes, Wildnerdpix), Wikipedia (Adrian Michael)

Library of Congress Cataloging-in-Publication Data
Gish, Melissa.
Brown bears / Melissa Gish.
p. cm. — (Living wild)
Includes bibliographical references and index.
Summary: A scientific look at brown bears, including their habitats, physical characteristics such as their coat, behaviors, relationships with humans, and elusiveness of the apex predators in the world today.
ISBN 978-1-60818-415-6
1. Brown bear—Juvenile literature. I. Title. II. Series: Living wild.

QL737.C27G57 2014
599.784—dc23   2013031808

CCSS: RI.5.1, 2, 3, 8; RST.6-8.1, 2, 5, 6, 8; RH.6-8.3, 4, 5, 6, 7, 8

First Edition
9 8 7 6 5 4 3 2 1

CREATIVE EDUCATION

BROWN BEARS

Melissa Gish

In Valdaysky National Park of northwestern Russia, a female brown bear emerges from a hole beneath a massive rock pile at the foot of a sloping hill.

In Valdaysky National Park of northwestern Russia, a female brown bear emerges from a hole beneath a massive rock pile at the foot of a sloping hill. She lifts her nose and inhales the cool spring air. Sensing no danger, she grunts softly to signal her two small cubs to follow her. The twins were born during the winter, and they obediently trot behind their mother as she steps forward, still groggy from her long winter's sleep. The bear leads her cubs to a slow-moving stream, where she drinks while her cubs swat at tiny fish that dart in the shallow water. The winter ice that covered the park's streams and lakes has melted, and shoots of grass and sedges rise from the water's edge. Keeping watch over her curious cubs, the mother bear begins to gorge on the tender greenery—her first meal in nearly six months.

WHERE IN THE WORLD THEY LIVE

■ **Syrian Bear**
parts of Eurasia and
the Middle East

□ **Eurasian Bear**
northern Europe,
Russia

■ **Kamchatka Bear**
Kamchatka
Peninsula

■ **Ussuri Bear**
northeastern
China, Russia

□ **Grizzly Bear**
North America

■ **Kodiak Bear**
Kodiak Archipelago

The 10 brown bear subspecies are scattered around the
Northern Hemisphere, with the largest populations found
in Russia. The colored dots represent native territories of
six brown bear subspecies that live in the wild today.

GIANTS OF THE NORTH

Brown bears are the most widely distributed bears in the world. They are found in dense forests, high plains, and Arctic tundras across North America, Europe, and Asia. The earliest bear ancestor, *Ursavus elmensis*, or the dawn bear, lived in Europe about 25 to 20 million years ago. No larger than a housecat or fox terrier, this animal was the forerunner of the many bear species that spread around the globe, each suited to its environment. Bears belong to the genus *Ursus*, which means "bear" in Latin. The eight species of modern bear are the sun bear of tropical Asia; the spectacled bear of South America; the sloth bear of India; the polar bear of the Arctic regions; the panda of China; the Asian black bear of southern Asia; the North American black bear; and the brown bear, of which there are 10 subspecies.

These subspecies are classified by geography. Eurasian and Syrian bears are found in Europe and northern Asia. East Siberian, Kamchatka, and Ussuri bears are found in Russia. The rare Gobi bear and Himalayan snow bear are found in the Asian lands for which they are named. The

Larger than modern bears, cave bears lived in Europe from about 2 million to 27,800 years ago.

Around 1 B.C., early Europeans used the word *bera* to describe the color brown. It later became the word for "bear."

Even from a distance, brown bears can be distinguished from black bears by their shoulder hump.

The largest brown bear ever, a 2,130-pound (966 kg) Kodiak named Clyde, died at the Dakota Zoo in Bismarck, North Dakota, in 1987.

grizzly bear inhabits the interior forests of North America; the Kodiak bear is a subspecies found only on the Kodiak Archipelago, which is a group of islands off the southern coast of Alaska; and coastal brown bears are found in habitats along ocean coastlines in Alaska and Russia.

A bear's coat, called pelage, varies greatly in color—even within species—from golden to brown and from gray to black. In North America, black and brown bear species are sometimes mistaken for each other, since black bears can be brown, and brown bears can be black. What sets brown bears apart from all their relatives is their distinctive shoulder hump. Powerful muscles under this hump give the brown bear superior strength in digging up rocks and tearing apart tree roots to find food. All brown bear subspecies have a shoulder hump.

Bears are mammals, animals that, with the exceptions of the egg-laying platypus and echidna, give birth to live young and produce milk to feed them. Like all mammals, bears are warm-blooded. This means that their bodies maintain a constant temperature that is usually warmer than their surroundings. With the exception of pandas, which are active in winter, bears

The Alutiiq people of
southern coastal Alaska call
the Kodiak bear taquka'aq,
their word for "bear."

Kodiak bears hunt for salmon in cold rivers and streams that average a temperature of 61 °F (16.1 °C) in summer.

develop a layer of thick fat just beneath the skin that protects against heat loss and provides nutrients through the winter, when most bears **hibernate**.

Male bears, which are called boars, are larger than females, called sows. Eurasian and grizzly bears are the smallest brown bear subspecies. In summer, when food is plentiful, males of these inland subspecies typically weigh around 800 pounds (363 kg), and females average 450 pounds (204 kg). Coastal brown bears grow larger than other subspecies because of the colder climate and fatty fish in their diets. Male Kamchatka and Kodiak bears can weigh as much as 1,500 pounds (680 kg) in summer and can tower up to 10 feet (3 m) tall when standing upright. Female Kodiaks generally weigh half as much as males and stand a few feet shorter. Although the Kodiak and its cousin the polar bear are roughly the same size, the polar bear spends most of its time in the water or on ice and so is considered a marine mammal. This makes the Kodiak the largest land-based predator in North America.

Brown bears are omnivorous, which means they eat both meat and vegetation. While they get most of their food from grazing on grass and berries and from

Bears are among the few wild animals known to suffer from cavities, and a diet too rich in sugar can cause tooth decay.

Brown bears have the largest brains of any land mammal relative to their size and can recognize people and other bears decades later.

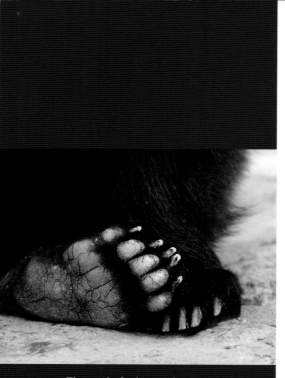

The pad of a brown bear paw is more elongated when compared with the rounded pad of a black bear.

scavenging dead animals, brown bears also hunt small mammals such as ground squirrels and marmots as well as large game such as deer, caribou, and moose. Coastal brown bears also capture fish—mostly salmon. In the summer and fall, bears may eat up to 90 pounds (40.8 kg) of food per day, doubling their body weight by the onset of winter.

The brown bear has 42 teeth that allow it to eat almost anything. Two pairs of long, sharp upper and lower canine teeth and six pairs of pointed incisors at the front of the mouth are used for ripping flesh. Eight pairs of small, flat teeth and five pairs of large molars along the sides of the jaw can crush and grind vegetation, nuts, and even bone. Brown bears have a powerful bite force. Even a great white shark's bite, at 690 pounds of pressure per square inch (48.5 kg/cm), or psi, is no match for a brown bear's bite at 1,200 psi (84.4 kg/cm).

Brown bears walk on the soles of the feet, a mammalian characteristic called plantigrade. This allows them to distribute their weight over a wide area and run swiftly—up to 35 miles (56.3 km) per hour—despite being so bulky. The bones in the legs and paws are thick, and each

Bears have weak distance vision and often stand up to better see objects that catch their attention.

GRIZZLY

COWARD,—of heroic size,
In whose lazy muscles lies
Strength we fear and yet despise;
Savage,—whose relentless tusks
Are content with acorn husks;
Robber,—whose exploits ne'er soared
O'er the bee's or squirrel's hoard;
Whiskered chin, and feeble nose,
Claws of steel on baby toes,—
Here, in solitude and shade,
Shambling, shuffling plantigrade,

Be thy courses undismayed!
Here, where Nature makes thy bed,
Let thy rude, half-human tread
Point to hidden Indian springs,
Lost in ferns and fragrant grasses,

Hovered o'er by timid wings,
Where the wood-duck lightly passes,
Where the wild bee holds her sweets,
Epicurean retreats,
Fit for thee, and better than
Fearful spoils of dangerous man.

In thy fat-jowled deviltry
Friar Tuck shall live in thee;
Thou mayest levy tithe and dole;
Thou shalt spread the woodland cheer,
From the pilgrim taking toll;
Match thy cunning with his fear;
Eat, and drink, and have thy fill;
Yet remain an outlaw still!

by Bret Harte (1836–1902)

paw has five digits ending in sharp claws that can be up to six inches (15.2 cm) long. The force that a bear can exert with its front paws is enormous. One swipe can behead a moose or crush its spine. Getting swatted full force by an adult brown bear would feel like getting hit by a car traveling down a city street.

Brown bears are powerful hunters, but they are even more skilled at scavenging because, like all bears, their sense of smell is highly developed. Bears often stand up on their hind legs to smell the scents carried by the wind. They can detect a **carcass** upwind from 20 miles (32.2 km) away. A bear's sense of smell is 7 times more sensitive than a bloodhound's and 21 times more sensitive than a human's. A bear's **olfactory system** is directly connected to the part of the brain that stores memories. This means that in addition to finding the food, bears can remember where they created shelters and stored food and where the best berries grow, year after year. Bears that are relocated often return to the places they once frequented by using their senses of smell and memory. Scientists also believe that hibernation may be triggered when brown bears smell changes in weather.

There have been no grizzly bears in California since the 1920s, but the animal is still featured on the state flag.

Before and during mating season is the time of year male bears most frequently rub on trees to leave scent marks.

THIS BEAR MEANS BUSINESS

The brown bear is a solitary animal, living alone in a particular area called its home range. The size of a brown bear's home range varies according to the amount of food resources available. The home ranges of male bears are four to six times larger than those of females. In Alaska's interior, a male brown bear's home range averages 521 square miles (1,349 sq km); in the Rocky Mountain regions of the United States and Canada, where food is more plentiful, the home range of a bear averages 347 square miles (900 sq km); and in coastal Alaska, where bears feed on abundant salmon, a bear needs only 10.5 square miles (27.2 sq km) on average.

Bears establish travel corridors, or regularly used paths, to patrol their home ranges. They mark their territory by rubbing their backs on and clawing trees, leaving a scent that communicates territory boundaries to other bears. The same trees are used year after year by generations of bears and are called "rubbing trees." Scents left behind on rubbing trees tell the age and gender of a bear and may also give clues as to a bear's health. Results from a study conducted in the early 2000s in British Columbia

Bears will investigate anything that smells or sounds unusual—generally to see if it is edible.

Brown bears can overturn 100-pound (45.4 kg) rocks, bite through cast iron skillets, and easily peel open car windshields.

A large bear will often push a smaller bear off a carcass or chase it relentlessly to steal the meal.

by ecologist Owen Nevin and from an ongoing study in northern Montana led by U.S. Geological Survey (USGS) ecologist Kate Kendall suggest that scent messages rubbed or clawed on trees may help bears who live close to one another recognize their neighbors and make decisions about whether to challenge them over food or mates.

A male typically allows two or three females' home ranges to overlap with his own, and, depending on the area, the home ranges of up to five male brown bears may also overlap. Bears generally tolerate each other, as they often pass through each other's home ranges along travel corridors, but a larger bear will always chase away competing smaller

bears from carcasses and other food sources. Younger bears generally avoid conflict by steering clear of older bears.

Brown bears are considered apex predators, meaning they are at the top of the **food chain**. They have no natural enemies other than each other. While bears typically prey on sick, injured, and very young or old animals, as much as 46 percent (or more, in some regions) of their diet is made up of vegetation, berries, and nuts. Bears are highly protective of their food. They often hide carcasses in dens or under shrubbery. This is called a food cache, and they will guard it fiercely. Bears also patrol areas where berries are plentiful, defending the bounty from potential thieves.

From the safety of wooden platforms, visitors to Alaska's Katmai National Park can watch bears feed at Brooks Falls.

In places where food is highly abundant (salmon-filled rivers, for example), bears are less competitive and have been observed feeding side by side, seemingly oblivious of each other.

Brown bears do not actively hunt humans, but when bears and humans do cross paths, bears will act to defend their territories and food caches—often with deadly force. Mother bears are particularly protective of their cubs and will often chase down any perceived threat. Bears prefer to avoid contact with humans as much as possible, yet dozens of people are injured and one to four people are killed each year in conflicts involving brown bears. Most people who fall victim to brown bears simply startle the bears as the animals are feeding or caring for cubs. However, there have been documented cases of brown bears dragging campers from their tents—usually in remote areas where bears may have never seen humans before. Most bears involved in attacks on humans are tracked down and killed in efforts to avoid repeat behavior. Mother bears that attack only to protect their cubs are usually not killed, since this is considered a natural defensive instinct and not an aggressive action.

Females give birth only once every three to five years, making the brown bear the second-slowest-reproducing mammal in North America (after the musk ox). Female brown bears are able to mate for only a three-week period sometime between May and July, depending on the weather. Male bears seek out females in and around their home ranges, and females typically mate with more than one male, which means they may produce a number of offspring from different fathers. Once bears mate, they go their separate ways again.

Because bears have such good hearing, wilderness hikers are advised to talk or sing to alert bears of their presence.

Bears are driven to locate a den site when they sense the coming of winter and diminishing food supplies.

Brown bears typically dig their dens into a north-facing slope so that the opening will be well covered with snow.

For bears, reproduction is influenced by climate and food supply. After the female bear's eggs are fertilized, they turn into balls of cells that float in the female's **uterus** for four to five months as the female gains enough weight to sustain her through the winter. Then, over a period of about 54 days, those cells develop into baby bears, called cubs. If the bear does not find enough food in the fall, her body resorbs the eggs, and no cubs are born that year.

If the female bear builds up a sufficient fat reserve, she will give birth to one to four cubs sometime between January and March, while she is hibernating in a den. A desirable den site is usually under a rock outcropping or dead tree roots, in the side of a hill, or inside a cave. Bear cubs are born blind, are nearly hairless, and weigh just nine-tenths of a pound (0.4 kg). However, newborns already have clawed front paws and a good sense of smell, which they use immediately. Clutching their mother's fur and following their noses, cubs make their way to their mother's underside, where they will nurse on her nutritious milk, gaining about 20 pounds (9 kg) by spring. By six months of age, bear cubs can weigh 55 pounds (25 kg).

Bear cubs stay with their mother for two to four years,

during which time they learn from her the best plants and berries to eat and how to catch fish and other small animals. At about five months old, the cubs begin to eat everything their mother eats, though they may continue to feed on their mother's milk for another two years. Cubs between the ages of four and six years old travel ever farther from their mother's home range until they establish territories of their own and begin breeding. Young bears on their own are most vulnerable to predators—particularly larger bears. At 10 or 11 years old, a bear is fully grown. Brown bears can live up to 35 years in the wild and 10 years longer in captivity.

Studies show that mother bears with four cubs typically lose two within the first year because protecting four is difficult.

Bear paintings made with red clay
in France's Chauvet Cave date to
approximately 32,000 years ago.

BROTHER BEARS

Since the earliest emergence of human **culture** in the Northern Hemisphere, brown bears have been important elements of people's spirituality and **mythology**. Some of the earliest existing evidence of the connection between bears and humans was discovered in 1957 at Régourdou Cave in southern France. Bones of brown bears were found to have been purposely arranged with artifacts and human remains. The 70,000-year-old site, considered one of the most important **Neanderthal** burial sites ever discovered, reveals that prehistoric people likely held brown bears in high regard as spiritual animals.

The first artwork ever created by humans includes paintings and etchings on cave walls. As the first modern humans spread across Europe, they incorporated brown bears in their artwork. Some of the earliest art depicting brown bears exists in southern France. A painting of a bear on a cave wall in Lascaux dates back 17,000 years, and the image of a bear etched into the rock of Combarelles Cave dates to 13,000 years ago. Three bears painted on walls of the Cave of Teyjat are about 10,000 years old.

Images of bears were carved into a Utah mountainside by San Rafael Fremont Indians between A.D. 600 and 1300.

Ursus etruscus, a brown bear ancestor, shared habitat with early humans and disappeared about 10,000 to 20,000 years ago.

In ancient Greece, female bears became symbols of motherhood based on the story of Callisto, a follower of the goddess Artemis. When Callisto had a son with the ruler of the gods, Zeus, Artemis turned Callisto into a bear and took away her son, Arcas. Years later, Arcas was hunting and nearly killed his own mother. To save them both, Zeus placed them in the heavens as the constellations Ursa Major and Ursa Minor, commonly called the Big Dipper and Little Dipper. In legends from Norway, the armies of ancient kings were made up of fierce warriors who dressed in bearskins. These warriors were called berserkers, a name taken from *beri*, the Old Norse word for "bear," and *serkr*, which means "shirt." Throughout Europe, the brown bear was known as the "king of the forest."

Images of the brown bear as a powerful and intelligent creature persisted throughout European fairy tales and folklore. In the 18th-century French fairy tale "Beauty and the Beast," a girl named Belle fell in love with a bear-like creature and discovered that he was a prince who was put under a magic spell. A century later, the tale "Snow White and Rose Red," by the Brothers Grimm, told the story of two sisters who befriended a bear and welcomed

him into their home. The family grew to love the bear and later discovered that the bear was really a prince who had fallen victim to an evil dwarf's magic spell. When the spell broke, Snow White married the prince, and Rose Red married the prince's brother.

One of the most famous fairy tales involving bears is "The Story of the Three Bears," which was first published in 1837 by the British poet Robert Southey. In the original story, an old woman invades the home of the three bears while they are out. She eats their breakfast, sits in their chairs, and sleeps in their beds before being startled by the bears' return and running away. In 1849,

The Pinwheel Galaxy, located near the "tail" of the constellation Ursa Major, can be seen with a telescope.

Just before they got into trouble, Yogi Bear often told his sidekick Boo-Boo, "I'm smarter than the average bear."

Joseph Cundall rewrote the story to make a little girl named Goldilocks the intruder in the bears' house.

Perhaps the most famous family of brown bears in contemporary literature can be found in a series of books written and illustrated by Jan and Stan Berenstain. Since their debut in the book *The Big Honey Hunt* in 1962, the Berenstain Bears have been featured in more than 300 books, 5 television specials, and 2 television series as well as a number of computer games and even a live stage musical. On television, the animated Yogi Bear and Boo-Boo Bear are two brown bears that live in the fictional Jellystone Park. Yogi, whose first appearance was on *The Huckleberry Hound Show* in 1958, has become one of cartoon history's most beloved figures. He can still be seen on the cable network Boomerang.

Another famous bear that makes frequent appearances on television and in print media is Smokey Bear, a mascot for the U.S. Forest Service. Smokey's slogan, "Only You Can Prevent Wildfires," reminds people about fire safety and the dangers of wildfires. Since the character of Smokey was created in 1944, he has undergone a number of changes in appearance but

Since 1952, money raised from sales of Smokey Bear merchandise has gone to support fire prevention education.

According to team lore, the mascot for the National Hockey League's Boston Bruins is a bear that loves hockey too much to hibernate.

remains one of the most recognizable brown bears in recent history.

While most fictional bears are portrayed as friendly, social creatures with human characteristics, real bears can be aggressive and dangerous, traits which make them perfect mascots for sports teams wanting to appear powerful and ferocious. The Chicago Bears professional football team has Staley Da Bear as its mascot and is well known for its players' bear-like tenacity. The National Basketball Association (NBA)'s Memphis Grizzlies first adopted Grizz the grizzly bear as its mascot in 1995, when the team was established in Vancouver, British Columbia. In 2011, Grizz was named the NBA's Mascot of the Year.

Brown University in Rhode Island kept a series of live brown bears as the school's mascot from 1905 until 1966, when it was determined that caging a bear beneath the stadium was no longer wise. Named Bruno, the mascot is today played by a human in a bear costume. The University of California, Berkeley, also had a live brown bear mascot from the late 1800s until 1941, when the first costume for the California Golden Bears mascot, Oski, was created from a baggy sweater and a pair of size 13-1/2 shoes painted gold.

Working with live brown bears is serious business, and in Hollywood, Doug and Lynne Seus are the experts everyone turns to when bears are needed for movies. In 1977, the Seuses adopted Bart the Bear, a Kodiak cub, and trained him to be an animal actor. Bart, who appeared in *The Bear* (1988), *White Fang* (1991), *The Edge* (1997), and 12 other films during his lifetime, stood 9.5 feet (2.9 m) tall and weighed 1,500 pounds (680 kg). Bart died of cancer in 2000, but the Seuses have other bears that act in movies today. Tank played Buster in 2011's *We Bought a Zoo*, and Bart the Bear 2 played Jerome the Bear in *Zookeeper* (2011). Bart's sister, Honey Bump, appeared in *Dr. Doolittle 2* (2001).

In 1304, the city of Bruges, Belgium, adopted an image featuring a lion and a brown bear as its official emblem.

Cubs can climb trees, but once their claws get long enough, older brown bears cannot climb trees.

KINGS OF THE FOREST

C urrently, brown bears are uncommon in most parts of Europe and are protected in only selected areas. As recently as the mid–1970s, brown bears were still being hunted extensively in North America. Fewer than 1,000 remained on the continent. In 1975, they were listed as a threatened animal on the U.S. Endangered Species List, which gave them legal protection from overhunting. In 2007, grizzlies were removed from the list in Yellowstone National Park, where their population is growing, but pressure from conservation groups led to the bear's return to the list in 2009.

With a worldwide brown bear population of about 200,000 individuals, some organizations such as the U.S. Fish and Wildlife Service and the Russian Hunting Agency are satisfied that the brown bear has made a complete comeback from the brink of **extinction**. In Europe, government conservation agencies from Norway to Spain disagree, citing that the recovery of a species is not simply indicated by population size. How widely animals are distributed and how successfully females are breeding—as well as the strength of **genetic** diversity

Brown bears lose up to two pounds (0.9 kg) of fat per day while hibernating, starting spring at 60 percent of their fall body weight.

within those populations—are important factors for lawmakers around the world to consider.

More than half of all the world's brown bears live in Russia. About 14,000 brown bears are found throughout parts of Europe and Asia, roughly 25,000 live in Canada, and about 33,000 inhabit the U.S. (mostly in Alaska). Most brown bear populations are scattered throughout their ranges in small pockets. For example, 25 to 30 brown bears exist in the Cantabrian Mountains in northern Spain, where brown bear population recovery efforts have been ongoing since 1975.

Much of the research conducted on smaller populations is designed to study the bears' movement within and around home ranges, their breeding habits, and other behaviors relating to the care of cubs. Studies also focus on the genetic makeup of populations. USGS researchers led by ecologist Kate Kendall monitor the roughly 765 grizzly bears living in a remote area of Glacier National Park in north-central Montana by gathering brown bear genetic samples in a uniquely non-invasive way.

Pieces of barbed wire are stretched across travel corridors or fixed onto the bark of known rubbing trees

in the grizzlies' habitat. Remote cameras are positioned to capture video of the bears that walk under or over the wire fence or rub against the trees. In scraping against the barbed wire, the bears painlessly leave behind bits of their fur. Any **follicles** still attached to the fur can be used to gather genetic information, and the video provides images that correspond with the bear that matches those genes. Researchers can then keep track of individual bears to aid in the management of the grizzly population in the park and help ensure that the population remains large

A mother brown bear's overriding concern is for the protection and education of her cubs.

Campers in bear country should remain aware that bears' curiosity may lead these animals to investigate campsites.

enough to sustain genetic diversity. If the population gets too small, then **inbreeding** can occur, causing health problems in future generations of bears.

More than 1,800 bears—the largest concentration of brown bears in the world—live on Admiralty Island in southeastern Alaska. The Tlingit (*KLING-it*) people of Alaska call the island Xootsnoowú (*KOOTS-noo-woo*), which means "fortress of the bears." Hunting is prohibited in some areas, and camping is limited, so the bears have not learned to associate humans with guns or food. The bears remain wild and therefore avoid humans. Bears—and humans—in other parts of Alaska are not so fortunate.

As humans continue to press into Alaskan wilderness areas—for reasons as varied as urban development and road construction, oil and gas exploration, and tourism and recreation—encounters with brown bears become inevitable. Bears in Alaska have killed fewer than 50 people in the past century, but close encounters with brown bears are increasing—a trend that has wildlife managers concerned. An increase in the use of camera phones is considered a major culprit in bear attacks. Tourists wanting to get close-up pictures of wildlife recklessly approach bears, which can provoke the animals to charge, maul, or even kill.

Research conducted on brown bears in Alaska provides wildlife managers with the tools they need to keep humans and bears safe from each other. Perhaps the foremost authority on coastal brown bears is LaVern Beier, who has been studying them for nearly 40 years and has handled more than 800 bears during his career with the Alaska Department of Fish and Game. He knows the dangers of studying North America's largest predator and always heads

When fishing, Kodiak bears attack quickly and often begin eating their prey while it is still alive.

Like all large predators, bears feed scavenging birds such as crows, ravens, and gulls, which take advantage of leftover food.

Although humans and bears have thousands of interactions each year, only a few result in human injury.

The more tourists try to see bears up-close, the less bears eat, which keeps them from gaining the necessary winter weight.

into the forest with a rifle, but he loves his work nonetheless. He has been attacked just four times—all because he was simply in the wrong place at the wrong time.

Beier uses **snares** that he developed to capture bears by the paw, immobilizing them so that he can tranquilize the bears to make them fall asleep. He places a collar holding a **Global Positioning System** (GPS) tracking device around the bear's neck. The GPS transmitter allows Beier to monitor the bear in the wild using data from **satellites**. Beier also clips a numbered tag in the bear's ear, takes measurements, and collects hair and blood for genetic identification. The whole process takes about 45 minutes. When the bear wakes up, it may be a little groggy but otherwise feels no effects.

New research is allowing brown bears to tell their own stories more directly as well. Biologist and Alaska native Becky Schwanke has so far collared nearly 140 brown bears in an area of Alaska wilderness and monitors them with the video cameras installed in each collar. The cameras automatically switch on for 20 seconds every 15 minutes for a month. Then the bears are recaptured and the cameras removed. The footage recovered from

these cameras has revealed the scavenging and hunting behaviors of bears in surprising detail and suggests that brown bears may hunt more frequently—killing just as often as they scavenge. This could be a behavior change resulting from climate change, human interference, or any number of other factors. Only by learning as much as we can about the secretive lives of brown bears can we begin to understand how to survive in their world and help them survive in ours.

Researchers work quickly to measure and tag brown bears so that the animals suffer as little stress as possible.

ANIMAL TALE: THE BEAR WARRIOR

Perhaps no other animal has inspired legends of strength and valor as much as the brown bear, which appears in traditional tales of virtually every culture in the Northern Hemisphere. One of the world's oldest written stories, composed sometime between the 8th and 11th centuries, is that of the Danish warrior Bödvar Bjarki (*BAWTH-var bee-YAR-kee*), known in Germanic folklore as Beowulf.

Long ago, Hrolf Kraki was king of Denmark. In a quest for power, the devious Queen Skuld of Norway ordered her army to invade Denmark so that she could seize Hrolf's throne. Hrolf had many warriors, but the bravest was Bödvar Bjarki.

The night before the battle with Queen Skuld's army, Hrolf's warriors gathered to plan their defense of the kingdom. They talked late into the night, preparing for the attack. But Bödvar, as if carried by an unseen hand, drifted away to his lodge and fell into a deep sleep.

The next morning, Queen Skuld's army charged Hrolf's fortress. Hrolf's warriors fought courageously, but they were no match for Queen Skuld's men. Hrolf wondered where Bödvar could be. No one could find him.

Then, just as it seemed that Queen Skuld's army would claim victory, an enormous brown bear, roaring like a thunderstorm, charged onto the battlefield. Hrolf's men watched as the bear, with paws as broad as a man's chest and claws as long as a man's hand, tore into Queen Skuld's front line, ripping her soldiers to pieces. It soon seemed that Hrolf's men would win the day.

Meanwhile, some of Hrolf's men continued looking for Bödvar. They finally found him, asleep, in his lodge. They shouted to wake him, but Bödvar was not easily roused. "Bödvar!" the men continued to shout, shaking the sleeping warrior. "We need you!"

On the battlefield, the enormous bear-warrior swept through Queen Skuld's army with the power of a tornado. With teeth gnashing and claws ripping, the bear crushed every man he touched. Blades broke in half against his chest, and blows glanced off his back. Queen Skuld's army struggled to defeat the mighty bear.

And then, as suddenly as he had appeared, the bear-warrior vanished.

Back in Bödvar's lodge, the warrior awoke. "What is it?" Bödvar asked, his head pounding. "I was dreaming—"

"The battle rages," Bödvar's comrades explained, "and we need you."

"I was dreaming that I was a bear—that I fought as a bear!"

It was true. As Bödvar had slept, his bear-spirit was awake and battling Queen Skuld's army with more ferocity than Bödvar would have been able to muster as a mere human. But in waking him, Bödvar's comrades had broken the spell, and Bödvar's bear-spirit evaporated like a dream.

Without the mighty bear-warrior, Hrolf's men were again no match for Queen Skuld's army, and soon the tide turned in her favor. Her men poured over Hrolf's defenses like a wave over sand, invading Hrolf's fortress and destroying his army. Queen Skuld took the crown of Denmark from Hrolf's sorrowful head.

As for Bödvar, the bear-warrior would return to fight another day—but that is another story.

GLOSSARY

carcass – the dead body of an animal

culture – the behaviors and characteristics of a particular group in a society that are similar and accepted as normal by that group

extinction – the act or process of becoming extinct; coming to an end or dying out

follicles – sleeves surrounding the roots of hairs that contain the cells that make the hairs grow

food chain – a system in nature in which living things are dependent on each other for food

genetic – relating to genes, the basic physical units of heredity

Global Positioning System – a system of satellites, computers, and other electronic devices that work together to determine the location of objects or living things that carry a trackable device

hibernate – to spend the winter in a sleeplike state in which breathing and heart rate slow down

inbreeding – the mating of individuals that are closely related; it can result in having offspring with health problems

mythology – a collection of myths, or popular, traditional beliefs or stories that explain how something came to be or that are associated with a person or object

Neanderthal – an extinct human species that lived in ice-age Europe about 200,000 to 35,000 years ago

olfactory system – the body's system of cells, nerves, and organs related to the sense of smell

satellites – mechanical devices launched into space; they may be designed to travel around Earth or toward other planets or the sun

snares – traps for animals that have a noose made of wire or rope

uterus – the organ in a female mammal's body where offspring develop before birth; another word for "womb"

SELECTED BIBLIOGRAPHY

Brunner, Bernd. *Bears: A Brief History*. Translated by Lori Lantz. New Haven, Conn.: Yale University Press, 2007.

Dolson, Sylvia. *Bear-ology: Fascinating Bear Facts, Tales & Trivia*. Masonville, Colo.: PixyJack Press, 2009.

International Association for Bear Research & Management. "Brown Bear." http://www.bearbiology.com/index.php?id=38.

San Diego Zoo. "San Diego Zoo Animals: Brown Bear." http://www.sandiegozoo.org/animalbytes/t-brown_bear.html.

Spillenger, Paul. *Bear Island*. DVD. Washington, D.C.: National Geographic Society, 2007.

Troyer, Will. *Into Brown Bear Country*. Fairbanks: University of Alaska Press, 2005.

Note: Every effort has been made to ensure that any websites listed above were active at the time of publication. However, because of the nature of the Internet, it is impossible to guarantee that these sites will remain active indefinitely or that their contents will not be altered.

Brown bears will go to great lengths—even walking underwater—to capture spawning salmon in Alaska's icy rivers.

INDEX